On the Four Noble Truths

On the Four Noble Truths

by Lama Yeshe Gyamtso

KTD Publications
Woodstock, New York

Published by:
KTD Publications
335 Meads Mountain Road
Woodstock, NY 12498, USA
www.KTDPublications.org

ISBN: 978-1-934608-45-6
LCCN: 20139430542013943054

This book is printed in the United States on acid-free recycled paper.

CONTENTS

INTRODUCTION

This little book is based on a seminar that I offered at Karma Triyana Dharmachakra Monastery in Woodstock, New York in the fall of 2006. The seminar took place over a weekend and consisted of five sessions, each devoted to one of five topics: the four noble truths, the four seals of the view, the four mindfulnesses, the four schools of Buddhist philosophy, and the four reliances.

The purpose of the seminar was to introduce the participants to several aspects of the Buddhist outlook. The participants were Buddhist practitioners, some of them quite seasoned. I therefore faced a challenge, in that I had to offer the material in such a way that it was both accessible to beginners and informative to long-standing practitioners. I have no idea if I succeeded on either score, but several people appear to have found this material helpful, so we have decided to offer it as a book.

As with every book published by KTD Publications, this book would never have seen the light of day without the encouragement and support of Peter van Deurzen, and the editorial and design genius of Maureen McNicholas. I am as always grateful to them both for their work and their friendship.

Yeshe Gyamtso

THE FOUR NOBLE TRUTHS

Much of what I am going to say will be based on Khenpo Ugyen Tendzin's excellent presentation of the four noble truths, which was his first teaching here at KTD. This occurred on the sacred occasion of the Buddha's first turning of the dharmachakra.

The Buddha's first sermon was on the four noble truths. The four noble truths are four truths that aryas or nobles realize. An arya is anyone who has achieved the path of seeing, which is the third of five main stages of the Buddhist path. The achievement of the path of seeing is brought about by insight into the four noble truths.

The four noble truths were the Buddha's first statement to his first five human disciples of the essence of his awakening. Earlier he had made a statement, with no witnesses, saying that what he had discovered upon his awakening was luminous, utterly tranquil, peaceful, beyond elaboration, inconceivable, and if he tried to explain it, no one would understand it. Finally, Brahma and Indra, we are told, convinced him to teach. The first human beings that he taught, about forty-nine days after his awakening, were the five ascetics that he had previously lived with. Initially they were unreceptive to him, but they became very receptive very quickly. Four of them achieved the state of an arhat during the first and second of his three repetitions and the last one during the third.

When we talk about the four noble truths nowadays, we do not expect the results to be quite so dramatic. We still have to begin with it any time we talk about Buddhism or study Buddhism because the four noble truths give you the best single outline that covers all Buddhist teachings. Now, as I just mentioned, the Buddha, in his first sermon, repeated the four noble truths three times. The first time, he said the first noble truth is the truth of suffering; the second noble truth is the truth of its cause; the third noble truth is the truth of cessation; and the fourth noble truth is the truth of the path. That was the first repetition.

He repeated them a second time and said suffering is to be known; its cause is to be abandoned; cessation is to be attained or achieved; the path is to be relied upon. That was the second repetition.

The third repetition, which is more rarely quoted than the first two, was: Other than suffering, there is nothing to be known. Other than its cause, there is nothing to be abandoned. Other than cessation, there is nothing to be achieved. Other than the path, there is nothing to be relied upon.

These three repetitions, as they are called, of the four

noble truths, are not just repetitions. They are the introduction to, the main presentation of, and the final conclusion to the Buddha's first and very concise presentation of what we now call Buddhism.

The first repetition, in which the Buddha just named the four truths, is easy to understand. With the Buddha's second repetition, we need to pay close attention to what he said about each of these things.

The First Noble Truth is the Truth of Suffering

Having introduced the idea of suffering by saying the first noble truth is suffering, implying that this is the first thing which is recognized as true by aryas or noble ones, he then said suffering is to be known. Now normally, when we think about suffering, we think suffering is to be abandoned, suffering is to be prevented, suffering is to be healed, or suffering is to be ignored. The Buddha did not say suffering is to be gotten rid of; he did not say suffering is to be ignored; he said suffering is to be known.

This is very important, because we spend a great deal of our lives trying to do exactly the opposite. We try to get rid of suffering directly; and if we cannot get rid of it, we try to ignore it. Generally speaking when you say that if you cannot change it you have to live with it, people understand that to mean if you cannot change it you should try to ignore it. The Buddha was saying you actually have to examine suffering; you have to pay more attention to suffering. Do not try to get rid of suffering. In fact, the third time, he made a very radical statement. He said other than suffering, there is nothing to be known. Now, this does not mean that there are no objects of knowledge that are not suffering in nature. It means that the one thing you need to really understand in order to be able to get rid of suffering is suffering. He says this because only through understanding your suffering can you come to understand its cause. If we look for a moment at the first two noble truths together, you will see that the Buddha's approach is to get rid of suffering by getting rid of its cause. Only by getting rid of the cause can you prevent the suffering. The reason why he put the suffering first, even though the suffering is the result of the cause and we normally think of results as coming second, is that in order to ascertain the cause, you must study, examine, and scrutinize your suffering.

This does not just mean studying the categories of suffering. Buddhism is very, very thorough in categorizing suffering. We have the four major and eight secondary types of human suffering; we have the sufferings of the six realms, as well as the three types of generic suffering; and there are further lists and supplements to the lists.

The point is that we must face up to our own suffering, because as long as we are in denial of how much suffering we are actually experiencing from moment to moment, we will neither be able to give it up, since we will not be motivated to do so, nor will we be able to understand where it comes from. To give you a very simple example, when you are suffering because of attachment to something you cannot have, as long as you distract yourself from that suffering you are not going to actually be able to cure the attachment. The only cure for attachment is letting go of it. There is no other cure.

None of the nine vehicles in Buddhism says you can keep attachment. They may have nine different ways to convince you to let go, but you have to let go. At some point, at some time, you have no choice. We will come back to that.

Not that I am good at it. Now, I have to say this: I am here as a translator, translating things that I have heard eminent teachers say, and I have had the good fortune to hear lots of eminent teachers say lots of profound things. I am doing my best to repeat their words, or if not their words, at least their message, as I understood it. I may be distorting it, but I am attempting not to do so. I am not claiming to possess any of the virtues that I am going to be describing this weekend. I have to say this, even though those of you who know me could not possibly imagine that I would ever claim to possess any virtue. I have, at times, been approached by people who heard me translate teachings about wonderful things that I am incapable of and they say, "How could someone as horrible as you sit there and translate such beautiful things?" In order to prevent that, I will now make a disclaimer: I do not possess any of these virtues.

What the Buddha was saying was that the only thing you have to really understand in order to come to a decisive resolution of the problem of suffering is suffering itself. An implication of that is that suffering contains within it evidence of its origin or its cause. If you look at suffering as a whole one common characteristic of all suffering is attachment. All suffering is accompanied by it, and you can see this for yourself if you look at your suffering. You can even do a little experiment; you can actually just pinch yourself and look at the pain and ask "Why do I not like this physical sensation?"

Suffering comes from attachment. We have all heard this a million times. Each and every one of us has heard or read that the cause of suffering is attachment more times than we can remember. I have heard it millions of times and I believe it. Why then do I not let go of attachment when I know it is the cause of suffering? Because I do not feel it intensely enough. It is not enough to believe it; it is not enough to believe that the Buddha said it; it is not enough to believe that the Karmapa said it; you have to feel the attachment within your own suffering. To the degree that you do, and only to that degree, will you be willing to let go. Because if it is merely a rumor, if it is merely a strongly held belief, your attachment will still be more powerful than your belief that you need to let go of it. So the Buddha began with suffering because we need to understand suffering. If we try to get rid of suffering directly, we just create more attachment because attachment is the desire not to suffer. Attachment to a specific thing is based upon the fact that we think that thing is going to make us feel better. Feeling better includes both pleasure and pain; less pain, more pleasure, both mental and physical. Deep down, we all want to feel better.

If you try to feel better, it does not work; it never works. Have you ever tried to have fun? You know, I have had a very persistent and irritating experience that when I go somewhere because I have to, like when I am traveling as a translator, I enjoy the place, the city, the town, whatever it is, immensely. If I then go there for fun, on vacation, I get very depressed because I am trying to have fun. You cannot have fun when you are trying. You cannot feel better by trying to feel better.

The Second Noble Truth is the Truth of the Cause of Suffering

Now, this one, like the truth of the path, gets put different ways in different contexts, but if we go back to basics, the most fundamental message, the Buddha's point, is that the cause of suffering is attachment. Attachment is treated differently in different vehicles within Buddhism, but attachment is the cause of suffering. You might ask why do I not say ignorance, since the twelve links of interdependence start with ignorance. Actually, from a Buddhist point of view, the most fundamental ignorance and the most fundamental attachment are the same thing, because the first moment of ignorance is, as Thrangu Rinpoche puts it, a moment of panic during which your mind is overwhelmed by the intensity of its own lucidity. That panic is ignorance, a state of being stunned, but its affect is attachment, and the two happen simultaneously. It is not coarse attachment in the sense of thinking about what you want, and it is not coarse ignorance in the sense of an active misapprehension. It is a state of being stunned and panicky at the same time. If we look at it this way, the cause of suffering is that our minds have two characteristics: one is emptiness, the absence of any kind of substantial entity; and the other is lucidity or cognition. Because the nature of cognition is unlimited (which is in fact because of its emptiness), it is overwhelming. Minds get overwhelmed by their own unlimited cognitive brilliance or lucidity, which causes us to be ignorant of their emptiness.

It is important to use the term *attachment* in this context because if we say belief in a self or imputation of a self and so on, the nature of language being what it is, it conveys the misapprehension that we are talking about an adopted belief, which we are not. We are talking about something that even the most primitive animals have. I have no idea what the difference is between my cognitive functioning and the cognitive functioning of an animal, of any type of animal, from big whales down to little bitty things, but I assume there is some substantial difference. Regardless of that, even though it appears that animals do not have many beliefs, they still have attachment. It is attachment that is fundamentally at issue here, and everything else comes from that. It is painful to talk about this. It would be less painful if we said the cause of suffering is karma and kleshas because you could purify your karma and hopefully by doing so you will be able to whittle away at your kleshas. Karma and kleshas are causes of suffering, but they come from attachment. It is trendier to say the cause of suffering is ignorance, because then you get the idea that you can turn on a light bulb and the ignorance will disappear. As Tilopa said, the ignorance of a thousand kalpas is dispelled by a single moment's illumination. This sounds very good, but so far we have not been able to do that. So we have to go back to the beginning and talk about the issue of attachment, because we suffer, really, through attachment. Now, what are we attached to? We are attached to the imputed self of persons and the imputed self of phenomena. We are attached to perceived characteristics. To put it more simply, we are attached to things as they were, or as we think they were. Why is that a problem? Because nothing is as it was; everything is always changing. Attachment causes suffering because attachment is always living in the past. We are attached to being what we were a moment ago, or a year ago, or ten years ago, and we are not; and we cannot prevent that. That is the fundamental cause of suffering. Now, of course, we also do terrible, foolish things because we are attached. All the foolish things we do, we do because we are attached to something that does not exist, this personal self, the selfhood, this state of stasis. Those acts, of course, cause us further suffering, but if we trace it back to the beginning, it starts with attachment.

Now, what did the Buddha actually say? He said in this first sermon that the second noble truth is the truth of the cause. The cause is to be abandoned. Other than the cause, there is nothing to be abandoned. Other than attachment, there is nothing to be abandoned. The notion that the abandonment of attachment is the only process required in order to eliminate suffering is the fundamental theme of all Buddhadharma. From the shravakayana all the way up to the atiyogayana and from the Vinaya all the way to Kalachakra, Buddhism is all about how to let go of attachment. Of course, it is also about transcending anger and ignorance and pride and jealousy, but they are all symptoms of attachment. In fact, we could say they are types of attachment.

We go so far as to define *dharma* as "freedom from attachment." Fruition dharma is the state of freedom from attachment. Dharma as a path is the process of gaining freedom from attachment. Dharma as teachings is instructions on how to gain freedom from attachment. When we take refuge in the dharma, we say, "I take refuge in the dharma, supreme among all that is free of attachment." Now, why do we say "supreme among all that is free of attachment?" Because there are states of temporary freedom from attachment that are lesser and ultimately not helpful. For example, states of unconsciousness, states of rebirth, states of hibernation, states of drug-induced intoxication where there is no manifest attachment. Dharma is the best form of nonattachment because it is complete. When practiced properly it leads to complete freedom from attachment.

I don't know if you believe in miracles or not; I'm open-minded about them because I refuse to not believe in something simply because I have not seen it. I have not seen any miracles, but all the miracles that we are told about are said to come from freedom from attachment.

In a sense, attachment is our only problem. By being attached we are missing something that is far superior to the nonexistent thing to which we are attached. Because by panicking in that way, and trying to freeze or stop everything, we are missing buddha nature. That's the real problem. In the liturgy called *Embodiment of the Three Jewels*, the line of confession in the seven branches says "I confess that I have not realized my mind to be buddha." Now why would you confess that? Normally, we confess things that we choose to do that we know are wrong. We have not chosen not to realize that our minds are buddha. Why then do we confess something that we appear to have no control over? Because it is the cause of all our problems. In freezing, in panicking, in being overwhelmed by the mind's cognitive lucidity, when we fail to see our minds as they are, we fail to see something so wondrous that if we saw it for even a moment, all attachment would be annihilated.

The good news about having to give up attachment is that you get something better. But if you think too much about getting something better, then it becomes just another object of attachment and it will not work.

The Third Noble Truth is the Truth of Cessation

We have had the result and cause of samsara; now we have the result and cause of nirvana. The Buddha said that the third noble truth is the truth of cessation; that cessation is to be achieved; and that other than cessation there is nothing to be achieved. Cessation is presented in different ways in different Buddhist vehicles, but what is common to all of them is that cessation means the cessation of suffering. As we know, that depends upon the cessation of the cause. In other words, the only thing you are trying to achieve is the cessation of attachment and thereby the cessation of suffering. This is important to understand, because any time that we practice Buddhism and are not working on attachment, are not attempting to achieve the cessation of attachment, we are cheating ourselves. We are trying to have our cake and eat it too. We have to remember what all of this starts out with, what the true issues are, and not avoid them. Sometimes we get so wrapped up in the corridors of Buddhism and techniques of Buddhism that we forget what the whole thing is really about.

The Fourth Noble Truth is the Truth of the Path

At this point the Buddha had talked about the need to understand suffering, the need to get rid of its cause, and that the only thing to achieve is the cessation of suffering through the cessation of its cause, but how do you do that? That is the fourth noble truth. He said that the fourth noble truth is the truth of the path; that the path is to be relied upon; and that other than the path there is nothing to be relied upon. Now, "other than the path there is nothing to be relied upon" does not mean "don't trust anybody." Relied upon doesn't mean that; it means that, other than the path, there are no tools you can use to get rid of attachment.

The Four Noble Truths in the Different Vehicles

To understand the different expressions or applications of the four noble truths in the different vehicles, you need to understand that the governing rule in all Buddhism—and this is something that has always been emphasized—is that the higher vehicles never actually contradict the lower vehicles. Nothing is taken away. They color them in; they fill them in. You must never think that the mahayana view or mahayana practice dispenses with the hinayana view or practice, or that the vajrayana view and practice dispenses with either the mahayana or hinayana. Anything that is true in the hinayana is still true, but it may not be the final truth or it may be explained in more detail in the higher vehicles. You can never think that you have outgrown the hinayana or the hinayana teachings.

It is easiest to summarize all Buddhist vehicles into those three. Of course, there are many vehicles, but we can talk most easily about the hinayana, which is the common vehicle; the mahayana, which is the great vehicle of the sutras, and the vajrayana, which is the great vehicle of the tantras.

I mentioned that when we take the vow of refuge according to the common vehicle, in taking the vow we define dharma as that which is supreme among all that is free of attachment. That definition of dharma applies to all vehicles.

In a sense, we can define dharma as supreme passionlessness, supreme freedom from attachment. That especially characterizes the common vehicle, the hinayana. The understanding of the practitioner of any form of the hinayana is that they have no choice but to let go of attachment. The idea of dharma is passionlessness, letting go, simply letting go. Of course, at any level, within any vehicle there is insight, there is tranquility, there are all sorts of things, but the common theme in the common vehicle, the hinayana, is letting go: letting go because you have no choice. You have to let go. Meditation in the common vehicle, as we will see tomorrow afternoon, is characterized by observing your experience in all arenas, physical, mental, emotional; and observing that you have to let go because you cannot hold on to anything. You cannot hold on to that which does not last, and none of the things we cling to last. We can, for purposes of understanding the four noble truths alone, define the hinayana view of dharma as letting go because you have no choice.

The mahayana is concerned with the achievement of perfect buddhahood for the sake of bringing all other beings to that state. This requires a compassionate motivation and the realization of emptiness. Through recognizing your own suffering you start to empathize with the suffering of others. Motivated by the desire to free others from suffering, you seek the realization of emptiness.

The vajrayana differs from the mahayana in one very important way. As Khenchen Thrangu Rinpoche puts it, "the mahayana of the sutras takes inferential reasoning as the path, and the vajrayana takes direct experience as the path." The end result of buddhahood is the same, but the means through which it is achieved and therefore the speed with which it is achieved are different.

You might ask, if vajrayana is the pursuit of a direct recognition of the nature of things, why do we seem to be engaging in all this fabrication, all this alteration? If the purpose is the direct recognition of the most fundamental nature of our being, an unalterable nature, why do we engage in alteration, why do we have all of these deities, and why all of this veneration of gurus? In other words, why does vajrayana involve so much worship? It seems to be all worship! Ninety percent of what we do around here seems to be worship. Well, that is because it is the key to direct recognition. Guru Rinpoche said that in the vajrayana the direct recognition of the nature of things is gained through the experience of purity—the experience of the purity of your own mind, your own body, and everything outside you, which means the environment and the minds and bodies of others. How do you experience that purity? Some people think that vajrayana practice is simply telling yourself that things are divine, that everything is divine. You do identify with the divine in vajrayana practice, but not by trying to convince yourself. There has to be something more than the mere use of the imagination.

As Guru Rinpoche said, "the source of the experience of purity or divinity is devotion." This is why we keep paintings of lineage gurus on the walls. The starting point of the authentic experience of purity has to be the recognition of the purity of another person, and for that to happen, it must be a person who is awakened enough that they can actually demonstrate the qualities of buddha nature in their demeanor.

One function of gurus is to demonstrate in their

physical and verbal demeanor the qualities of buddha nature. That produces devotion and once you identify the sacred, the divine, in the guru, then you know what it looks like, so to speak. You can then find it in yourself and in your world.

We often glimpse something extraordinary in one or another of our teachers. That glimpse is the beginning of the journey toward the direct recognition of buddha nature through the experience of purity, which arises from devotion. How do we gain devotion? Through faith. Yet the Buddha told us to question everything. When should we question, and when should we trust?

In the beginning you must question, otherwise you will not develop genuine faith, but when you are actually building faith, if you keep on questioning too much, if your open-minded skepticism becomes prejudicial skepticism, as it often does, then you undermine your faith in every moment. So there have to be phases in our growth. Questioning is like excavation; faith is like the construction of a building. Without excavation, there will be no foundation. Once the foundation has been dug and construction has begun, you don't keep tearing what you have built back down. That is what we do when we have not gained certainty through the initial period of healthy skepticism and we carry the habit of doubt into the phase of our practice where we need to have faith. It would be like digging the foundation and then still trying to dig the foundation while you are supposed to be constructing the building.

In order to gain direct recognition of buddha nature,

your mind's nature, vajra nature, whatever you want to call it, you need to start with faith in your guru. The guru has to be authentic. If he or she is not authentic, you will become obsessed with his or her defects. Although the guru does not have to be perfect, the guru has to be able to demonstrate to you the existence of buddha nature. Your side is to have faith, open-mindedness. You cannot be skeptical. If you are still skeptical by the time you are relating to your guru in the vajrayana way, then even if the guru proves beyond a doubt that the nature of all appearances is sacred or divine, you might believe it for a moment, but afterwards you'll convince yourself that it never happened. The reason why vajrayana, which is concerned with the direct recognition of the mind's nature, involves so much worship is the need for faith.

How the Three Vehicles Look at the Four Noble Truths

The common vehicle, the hinayana, describes suffering in great detail. The cause of suffering is understood in the common vehicle, in the hinayana, to be attachment of all kinds, which must therefore be relinquished; to be kleshas, which are all symptoms of attachment; and to be karmas, the actions we engage in overpowered by kleshas. The emphasis is on the attachment to the personal self as the cause of suffering because the imputation of a personal self, attachment to the personal self, is what keeps us in samsara. Attachment to the self of phenomena is what prevents us from achieving omniscient awakening, but it does not prevent us from escaping samsara, which is the principal goal of the common vehicle.

Cessation in the hinayana is understood to be the end of experience, at least experience as we know it. In the mahayana and vajrayana it is taught that mind never ends.

The path in the common vehicle, the hinayana, consists of the three trainings. In more detail, we could say that the Buddhist path consists of the thirty-seven factors of awakening, and that is true for all Buddhist vehicles. The noble eightfold path is the last eight of them. In all Buddhist vehicles the path can be divided into the thirty-seven factors of awakening. Tomorrow afternoon we will be looking at the first four of them because they constitute the actual practice of a beginner, which means a person on the lesser path of accumulation, the first of the five paths.

The practice of the common vehicle consists of three aspects of training: morality, samadhi, and knowledge. Morality means exactly what it sounds like: behaving well, behaving properly. There are two reasons to behave well. One is because you do not want others to suffer; that motivation is present in all vehicles. The other is because you do not want to accumulate karma that will keep you suffering in samsara.

The training of samadhi is the cultivation of tranquility and insight through the practice of meditation. The training of knowledge is the cultivation of recognition of your mind's nature. In the common vehicle, knowledge is mainly the recognition or the knowledge of selflessness. In the mahayana, it is the knowledge of emptiness, and in the vajrayana, of the nature of mind. These are actually the same thing. Selflessness, emptiness, and the nature of mind are the same thing viewed in different ways.

The mahayana looks at suffering in the same way, except that there is a greater emphasis on understanding the suffering of others, and resolving to free them from suffering and its causes. The mahayana understanding of the cause of suffering is that it is caused fundamentally by ignorance. The mahayana understanding of cessation is that it is the cessation of ignorance, not the cessation of cognitive experience. It is the nondwelling nirvana of a buddha. From a mahayana point of view, any state of cessation that is not omniscient awakening is only temporary and will involve some kind of return to the path. If you want to know more about that, read the first chapter of Gampopa's *Jewel Ornament of Liberation.*

The mahayana path includes the three trainings, but they are given the epithet "superior": superior training in morality, superior training in samadhi, and superior training in knowledge. What makes them superior? The motivation of bodhichitta. Your morality is superior to that of the common vehicle because it is not simply that you behave well because you do not want to be a nuisance and do not want to suffer as a result of your actions. You behave well because you want to bring all beings to a state of perfect and omniscient awakening and you cannot even maintain that motivation, let alone fulfill it, without behaving well. This is important. Your vow is to achieve buddhahood for the benefit of all beings and, most importantly, not to give up the intention to achieve it for their benefit. You may say, "Even if I do something bad, I have not given up my intention." Is that true? When you do something bad (and I have done lots of bad things), does that not weaken your intention? How real is your intention to walk somewhere if you are walking in the opposite direction? How real is an intention that is infected with that level of procrastination? That is why it is said in the mahayana that bodhisattvas with infractions will be long delayed in achieving the levels, the bhumis. So from the mahayana point of view, immorality is problematic not only because it hurts others, but because it delays your awakening. That is hurting others in a really big way: you are depriving them of a buddha.

Mahayana samadhi is distinct from that of the common vehicle in that it is the integration of compassion with the realization of emptiness. The training of knowledge in the mahayana is aimed at the realization of the emptiness of all things, because that realization is necessary for the achievement of buddhahood.

The vajrayana view of suffering, the cause of suffering, and the cessation of suffering is not too different from that of the mahayana. The vajrayana path, however, is the cultivation of the direct experience of the nature of things by experiencing it as the nature of one's mind. This depends primarily on devotion to your guru. It is therefore said, "In the beginning you imagine your guru to be a buddha. In the middle you understand that your guru is a buddha.

In the end you realize that your mind is buddha."

Those are the three repetitions of the four noble truths, as they were first taught by the Buddha and then as viewed in the three vehicles. Obviously, this has been a very brief summary of this subject.

Questions

STUDENT: Early on you said that we need to develop insight into our own suffering. I was curious as to how would one go about doing that.

LAMA YESHE GYAMTSO: The idea of developing compassionate insight through an awareness of your own suffering is that compassion comes from being able to empathize with someone else when you see them suffering. In order to do that, you have to recollect the experience of suffering. If you ever totally lose touch with what suffering is like, you become less concerned with the suffering of others because you forget how bad it is. Insight into your own suffering would be the recognition that the common characteristic of all suffering is attachment. When we talk about the cause or origin of suffering, we think of it as a karmic cause, such as I did this in that life and so in this life I am ill or poor, but the fundamental reason we suffer is because we are stuck on stuff and we cannot let go. Regardless of the circumstances into which you have been born, why does it bother you? Because of attachment.

We suffer constantly in one way or another and we always identify the individual characteristics of each suffering and then define suffering as that. Suffering is loss, suffering is anxiety, suffering is physical pain, suffering is poverty. These are all suffering, but why are they suffering? Because we are attached. The only solution is letting go, as hard as it is. Now, you cannot just let go because you want to; you cannot do it through an act of will. We need tools. We need a process; but we cannot ever lose track of the fact that the purpose of these tools is to help us to let go.

One of the most traditional Buddhist analogies for this is the way they used to catch monkeys. You take a jar and you put a peach or something else that monkeys like in the jar, but you make sure that the opening of the jar is too small for the monkey to pull his hand out if he is holding onto the thing, the fruit or whatever it is; he can get his hand in if his hand is empty, but he can't pull his hand out if he is holding onto something. Then you anchor the jar somehow to the ground. The monkey will not leave the jar because he can't get his hand out, since he won't let go of the desired object. We are like that. All we have to do is let go and we will be free, but we don't. The other thing that needs to be mentioned, of course, is that the thing that we're holding onto doesn't really exist.

STUDENT: I don't really have a question, but can you repeat the quote from Thrangu Rinpoche, what was said about the overwhelming panic.

LAMA YESHE GYAMTSO: Well, the way Thrangu Rinpoche explains it, the mind has two main qualities or characteristics: one is its emptiness and the other is its cognitive lucidity. Because the cognitive lucidity is empty, it is unlimited in its potential brilliance or intensity. Because the mind's lucidity is overwhelmingly brilliant, the mind, overwhelmed by its own cognitive lucidity, becomes ignorant of its own emptiness. It thereafter mistakes that emptiness to be a self and the cognitive lucidity to be other. That means that what you experience, the cognitive lucidity, is seen as separate from what experiences it.

STUDENT: I don't know whether this can be answered without omniscient knowledge, but I know that I've heard you say a few words about it at some point and maybe you could try to say it again. You said that in the mahayana and vajrayana it is taught that experience never ends. Could you say something more about that?

LAMA YESHE GYAMTSO: I'm simply repeating what I've been told. In the hinayana sutras, it's implied that the state of nirvana is the cessation of all experience, that the person is snuffed out like a candle flame. The mahayana belief is that, although an arhat might experience a prolonged period devoid of experience, it's temporary, and they have not really ceased to experience. They are just temporarily experiencing no experience. Eventually a Buddha is going to awaken them from that state and say, "Venerable one, the nirvana you have achieved is not nirvana; gaze upon the form of the tathagatha and understand it!" and so on. This is explained in the *Jewel Ornament*. We believe that is what an arhat experiences. Bodhisattvas, of course, are still evermore conscious as their path increases and when you achieve buddhahood, through either the mahayana or vajrayana, its state is indescribable, but it is not an absence of wisdom. In the twentieth or twenty-first chapter of the *Jewel Ornament of Liberation*, Gampopa briefly addresses the controversy between those who present buddhahood, because it is devoid of effort and thought, as a state without experience, and those who say it possesses experience. He gives different points of view and then Milarepa's solution to the question. When he asked Milarepa "Do buddhas experience or not?" Milarepa said, "Leave this old man alone! Look at your mind; it's like that." So it is in a sense not something that can really be understood or discussed.

THE FOUR SEALS OF THE VIEW

We are going to look at the four seals of the view, which are an important set of Buddhist principles or beliefs. They are called "seals of the view" because the Buddha said that the definition of a Buddhist is someone who accepts those four things. They are imprints, marks, or seals of a Buddhist view

Although these are connected with all of the four noble truths, they are most closely connected with the first truth, the truth of suffering. When someone achieves the path of seeing, they achieve sixteenfold insight into the four noble truths. The insight into the truth of suffering is the recognition of four marks or characteristics of things. The four seals of the view more or less correspond to these, so we could say that they are aspects of the truth of suffering. The reason why these are called seals is that the Buddha is said to have said that these are the defining parameters of a Buddhist view. In other words anyone who accepts these four ideas is, by the Buddha's definition, a Buddhist, and a follower of his teaching.

The four seals are impermanence, suffering, selflessness, and nirvana. The four seals are very much connected to the truth of suffering; they are, in a sense, what is to be known about suffering. The four mindfulnesses are the means through which you begin to abandon the cause of suffering. The four views are primarily views of cessation. The four reliances are how to find a practical path.

Impermanence

The first of the four seals is impermanence. The text for this is "All composites are impermanent." "All" means each and every one, without exception. A composite is any thing that is made up of more than one thing. This means any physical thing that has parts and any mental thing or state that has parts. Another way to understand composites is anything that is produced by causes and conditions. If anything is made up of more than one thing and if it is produced by causes and conditions, it is impermanent.

Now, what is meant by saying that a thing is impermanent? Two things are meant; and they are, in a sense, equally important. The more obvious meaning of impermanence is that the thing will not last forever, and that is what we call coarse or gross impermanence. The coarse or gross impermanence of every composite thing is that at some point it is not going to be there anymore. This is true of biological life forms such as ourselves; it is true of all substantial things that we know; and it is true of mental states as well. But if you think about coarse impermanence, you might wonder, "Why would things persist for a certain period of time and then all of a sudden fall apart? That doesn't make any sense." You're right; it doesn't make any sense. The truth of the matter is they do not persist through time; they are constantly changing, and that is the other aspect of impermanence: subtle impermanence. To simplify coarse and subtle impermanence, you can say that coarse impermanence is destruction and subtle impermanence is change. All composites are subject to constant change and eventual destruction or disappearance, but the destruction is really caused by the constant change that things undergo. For example, we think of death as a unique event in a person's life. Death can be caused by immediate circumstances, but it is also the inevitable culmination of the gradual breakdown of your body. We have been approaching death ever since we were conceived. Even as our embryonic bodies developed, we were aging and therefore approaching death. This is not in any way to minimize the agony of death, but it doesn't happen in a vacuum. In the same way, when you observe that something breaks suddenly, it breaks because of a process, because of various circumstances. Fundamentally, it breaks because it can break; it breaks because it is not really one thing to begin with; it is made up of different bits and those bits can be separated under certain circumstances. Therefore subtle impermanence is important.

When it is said that composites are constantly undergoing change, or constantly changing, does this mean that they ever remain exactly the same for any period of time? According to Buddhism, there is no unit of time, regardless of how brief it may be, during which a composite thing is in stasis, during which it remains in a state that is identical at the end of that unit of time to what it was at the beginning of that unit of time.

If things are not the same for any amount of time or duration, things never really retain the characteristics that we impute to them. This means that every time we think of a thing, we are thinking of a thing that no longer exists. When you look at something and think about it, you are actually thinking about a thing that no longer exists. All thoughts about any object of experience are, at best, based on a memory of that object in the past. If the object is one that does not change noticeably, this does not seem to affect our lives. When, however, the object is our minds or our bodies, our clinging to the past and expecting things to be what they were in the past causes us to suffer. Our minds and bodies are always changing. The external world is also always changing, but our worst problem appears to be how we relate to our own mind and the contents of our mind. We become rigid and fixed because we falsely believe on an instinctual level that whatever our mind was like before, it must be the same way now. This clinging to permanence is the immediate condition for the maintenance of habits. If someone becomes free from this misapprehension of the permanence of mental states, we are taught, they become free from habits.

Habits are unnatural. Buddhists use the term *natural* to mean "our true nature, our buddha nature." Everything that is not an attribute of buddha nature is unnatural. Habits seem natural to us because we have been messed up for so long. For example, it seems natural for us to be addicted to all kinds of things, mental and substantial. It seems natural for us to get angry; but while it seems natural for us to do that, these things are not truly natural to us. They are natural to us only in the way that when you are ill, it is natural to feel sick, although sickness is not a natural condition. Therefore there has to be some kind of persistent illusion that maintains habits. Part of that is the misapprehension of permanence. That is why understanding impermanence is so germane to the understanding of suffering. The expectation that things will be what they were in the past is thoroughly mistaken. It is impossible that they could be as they were, even if "were" refers to a moment ago. That mistaken expectation maintains habits and therefore causes much of our suffering.

Suffering

The second seal is suffering. "All that is defiled brings suffering." The definition of defilement here is "kleshas," including the misapprehension of permanence. Defiled mental states are all founded on that freeze, that panic that we talked about last night. Once you are attempting to stop time, to stop the world, once you are unwittingly attempting to prolong the past, which we do constantly, you are going to suffer. There are no two ways about it. There is no possibility that you are not going to suffer once you do that because you are at odds with reality. You are expecting things to be other than they are. The most common descriptions of suffering are the four sufferings and the three sufferings.

The Four Sufferings

The four sufferings are sometimes said to be sufferings specifically characteristic of the human state, of being human. They are also often said to be the generic sufferings of any kind of sentient being.

We'll go through them first because they are sufferings we know about and they are also very much connected with impermanence; they are birth, aging, sickness, and death. The suffering of birth is twofold: it is the difficulty of birth, the fact that it is a difficult process for all involved; and secondly, it plunges you into an unfriendly and hazardous environment. Because of modern medicine, birth is obviously a lot less hazardous than it used to be; but it is still a very dangerous thing and if you are going to be alive, you cannot avoid it; one way or another, you have got to be born. However you are born, you have got to go through some kind of birth process, and that is always dangerous. This may seem so obvious that you may wonder why we need to point it out. The answer is just to show that from the very start of our lives, there are all kinds of things that potentially can go wrong.

Then we have aging. Aging is the gradual reduction of your faculties, the degeneration of your body. Aging just by itself is difficult, and in addition, it is also the approach of inevitable death.

The third suffering is sickness. Sickness in the broadest sense simply means the breakdown of the body. It can be caused by illness or by accident and so on.

The fourth suffering is death. There are two things that are very important to remember about death. The first thing is the inevitability of death. We know, without any question whatsoever, that we are going to die. The second thing is that we have no idea when it will happen. We can say, with reasonable certainty, that one hundred years from today every single person in this room right now will be dead. Aside from that, we have no idea when we are going to die. This roof could fall in, killing all of us; any one of us could have a heart attack or a stroke and drop dead right on the spot; anything could happen. You could already have been struck by the illness that is going to cause your death without your knowing it. We have no way to know. There is sometimes some warning; a lot of times there is no warning. We do not know when we will die or what will cause our deaths.

The Three Sufferings

The three sufferings are another way of dividing suffering. The first is the suffering of suffering. The suffering of suffering is the experience of physical or mental pain of any kind.

Second is the suffering of change. This is the process by which pleasant circumstances change into unpleasant ones. This is actually the suffering that is embedded within pleasure. This is not to say that pleasure is not pleasure. It is, but pleasure contains suffering embedded within it because it cannot last. If you feel good, at some point you are going to feel bad. It is absolutely certain. This is not to say that the pleasure is the only cause of the pain; the pleasure is the cause of part of the pain, which is our feeling of contrast.

The third suffering is the pervasive suffering of the transitory composite. Because all composite situations are constantly falling apart, there is always some kind of suffering, even if you don't notice it. As Lord Gampopa wrote in the *Jewel Ornament of Liberation*, it is only the first kind that we experience as suffering. Afflicted sentient beings perceive the suffering of suffering as painful sensations, the suffering of change as pleasant sensations, and the pervasive suffering of the transitory composite as neutral sensations. That is suffering, the second of the four seals.

Selflessness

The text says, "All dharmas are selfless and empty." Selfless in colloquial English means unselfish; that is not what it means in this context. Here selfless means without true existence, without a self. In order to understand selflessness, we need to understand how Buddhists define a self, especially since we talk of both the self of persons and the self of phenomena; how can phenomena, things, dharmas, have a self? Let us look at the self of persons, first of all, and then at the self of phenomena.

The first thing to understand about the self of persons is that there isn't one; there never has been. The purpose of Buddhist practice is not to get rid of the self; there is no self. If there were a self, we could not get rid of it. Buddhist practice is not about getting rid of the self. Nor is it actually about the disintegration of the personality. It is about letting go of a very, very, very bad habit that we have, the very, very, very worst habit that anyone could have, and we all have it. It is a habit, more than a belief, a habit that was created by that first moment of panic, that first moment of ignorance. The habit causes our beliefs, but it is not the same as our beliefs. The habit is to assume, feel, and believe that we are permanent, unitary, and independent.

Independent here means "unchanging," because if you are independent, nothing can cause change. Now, you might say that you don't believe that. It doesn't matter what you believe. Animals don't believe anything and yet they have the same habit. Because we assume ourselves to be permanent, which we are not, we expect ourselves to remain the same through time and we're disappointed and disillusioned when we do not. Because we assume ourselves to be unitary, we feel as though we are one centralized entity that is inherently separate from everything around us. But we are not. We are made up of our experiences, our influences, our thoughts, all sorts of things; all of that is part of us.

We also assume that we are independent. In other words, we feel on an instinctual level that because we are separate from everything around us, our existence, our unchanging and permanent existence as a self, is independent. But we are not independent; we are influenced by every experience, every newly acquired bit of information, every cup of coffee, every breath of air; we're constantly changing what's in our minds. Even if you say "That's not me that's changing," it is you. "You" includes all of that. You are not a unit that can be separated from your experience. Generally speaking, there are two main bases of imputation for the self; there are two things that we identify with as "I" or "me". These are our bodies and our minds. Sometimes we think "I am my body." Sometimes we think "I am my mind and I inhabit my body; the body is a tool or residence of the mind and the mind is the self." Sometimes we think "I am both," that what I call "I" or "me" is a combination of body and mind.

The body is not the self because it does not possess the characteristics that we impute to the self, that we assume the self to have. The body is not permanent or unitary or independent or unchanging. The mind is not the self because the mind is not permanent, in the sense of unchanging; it is not unitary; and it is certainly not independent. You might say "What about the subtle mind, the basic mind that never changes, the mere continuity of experience? That is the self." Even that mere continuity of experience does not possess the characteristics we impute to it. You might say "I impute no characteristics to it, except the mere continuity of experience." Yet you do impute characteristics to it on an instinctual level; otherwise you would not have the instinct of self-preservation. If you did not believe on some level that you and everything you experience, your world, were inherently separate, then you would not seek to protect yourself at the expense of the world around you. You do; you protect everything that you regard as "I," "me," or "mine." We all do.

There is nothing other than the body and the mind that can serve as a reasonable basis for the imputation of the self, so if neither the body nor the mind is the self, there can be no personal self. Generally speaking, we regard the self as inhabiting the area from our skin inward. That's the actual territory of "I" or "me." Everything outside of that we regard as "not me." It may be mine or it may be not mine, but it's not me. Sometimes this changes. For example, if you have a limb removed, that limb was certainly within your skin; after its removal, is it still you or is it not you? We can use a tooth as an example; if you have a tooth removed, is that tooth you or not you? Before it was removed, was it you or wasn't it you? You might say "It was me before it was removed, but is not me once it has been extracted." Can something be you at one moment and not you at another? If part of you can be removed, does that mean that your self has parts? If so, it is not indivisible or unchanging.

The second aspect of selflessness is the selflessness of

things in general. The statement that dharmas are selfless means that they do not inherently possess the characteristics that we impute to them. There are two categories of things in this regard. These are appearances, which include everything we experience through any of our five senses; and thoughts, which include everything we experience with our minds. Of course, we experience everything with our minds; but some of what we experience is based upon our senses, and some of it is not.

Do appearances exist outside our experience of them? Many people would say that what we see, hear, smell, taste, and feel only exists in our senses and minds, but that there must be hidden objective bases that interact with our senses for appearances to arise. For example, although it is easy to demonstrate that my perception of color is in part due to my eyes and mind, many people would say that there must be something "out there" that interacts with my eyes for my perception of color to occur. In other words, many people would say that what I see may not exist but there must be something out there causing me to see it. This is the proposition of a hidden objective basis of perception, and we will return to this idea tomorrow afternoon.

Do thoughts have true existence, independent existence, or not? Well, we can argue about that until we're blue in the face, but the best way is to look at your thoughts. When you're sitting in meditation and a thought arises, rather than looking at the content of the thought, being swept away by the thought, or attempting to suppress or get rid of it, look at the thought itself. If you do it enough times, you will come to a decisive conclusion about whether or not thoughts have true or independent existence.

Nirvana

It is said, "Only nirvana is peace." *Nirvana* means the "transcendence of misery." There are two types of nirvana: the nirvana of an arhat and the nondwelling nirvana of a buddha. The nirvana of an arhat is what happens when someone eradicates all kleshas and gets rid of the fixation on the personal self, but does not eradicate all ignorance and does not realize the selflessness of phenomena, or at least not completely. We are told that such a person, after their death, will for a long time remain in a state that is more or less devoid of experience. They will eventually be aroused from that state by a Buddha; you can read about this in the *Jewel Ornament of Liberation*. The person will never again be born in samsara, but it will take them a long time to complete the rest of the path to full awakening because, having eradicated the kleshas, they can no longer take rebirth.

Nondwelling nirvana is the state of buddhahood. As we discussed last night, it is almost impossible to characterize it. It seems incorrect to say that it is a state without experience because that is tantamount to saying the appearance of a buddha is merely an illusion or hallucination on the part of the perceiver. On the other hand, to say that it is a state with experience implies ordinary experience, which, we are told, buddhahood does not possess. Buddhahood is inconceivable because it is outside the realm of any experience that we have known. It is the state of perfection, and imperfection is all we know.

Those are the four seals: All composites are impermanent; all that is defiled brings suffering; all things are selfless; and only nirvana is peace. These can be understood as four topics within the truth of suffering. Impermanence is a condition for suffering; defilement is the cause of suffering; neither the person who suffers nor the suffering they undergo possess a self; and, until you achieve nirvana, there will always be suffering.

Questions

STUDENT: Touching upon what you just said, if there is no permanent self, then what is it that continues on the birth cycle? What is it that continues onward?

LAMA YESHE GYAMTSO: It is a continuity of experience that cannot reasonably be called a self, in the definition of *self* that we are using here, because it is constantly changing. It is tricky to talk about this because when you say there is no self it implies that the mind is just produced by physical causes and conditions and therefore will disappear when you die. That's not what Buddhists mean. The appearance of a self is causality mistaken to be identity. Because of causality, we are reborn, but the consciousness that undergoes rebirth is constantly changing.

Think about you, right now, and think about you when

you were eight years old. Now, to say you are not the same person you were when you were eight years old is fine, but you certainly have a unique relationship with that eight-year-old, because you have memories from that age that no one else has. Even if other people have the same memories, they have them from a different perspective. You have a unique perspective on your history. Only you experience the memories, habits, and karmic imprints of what you did and experienced when you were eight.

On the other hand, beyond that continuity, there is absolutely no characteristic whatsoever that you can separate or isolate from all of the elements of experience that make you up and say, "This is me; this is what is not changing." Your body is not the body you had when you were eight. Your mind is not the mind you had when you were eight. You know things you didn't know then, and you've forgotten things you knew then. Your personality is different. You're taller than you were then. You may say, "My body and mind have changed, but I had brown eyes then, and I have brown eyes now. I had black hair then and I have black hair now. If I weren't me, I might have green hair or purple hair or yellow hair." Your brown eyes and black hair, however, are results of the eyes and hair you had then, not the same eyes and same hair.

That is a mistake we often make: mistaking causality for identity. You are the result of what you were at the age of eight; you are not the same. For example, when we say that you have the same DNA, it means that your current DNA is a result of your past DNA. It does not mean that the particles or cells making up your body today are the same ones that made up your body when you were eight. It's like an acorn and an oak tree. The acorn is not the oak tree; the oak tree is not the acorn; the oak tree is the result of the acorn. There is a unique connection between the acorn and the oak tree. Acorns don't grow into tigers and tiger fetuses don't grow into oak trees. Nevertheless an acorn is not the same thing as an oak tree; its characteristics are distinct. That is the idea.

THE FOUR MINDFULNESSES

We have looked at the four noble truths and how they are, in a sense, the outline of all the Buddha's teaching, as well as the first sermon he gave. We have also looked at the four seals of the view, which are primarily connected with the first of the four truths, the truth of suffering, which is what is to be known or understood. The second noble truth, the truth of the origin or cause of suffering, and the fourth noble truth, the truth of the path, are connected in that the path is the process of abandoning the cause of suffering.

The Buddhist path is usually divided into five phases: the path of accumulation, the path of juncture, the path of seeing, the path of meditation, and the path beyond training. The practices that make up these five paths are called the thirty-seven factors of awakening. The five paths are further subdivided; the path of accumulation, for example, is divided into three levels. On the first of the three levels of the path of accumulation, usually called the lesser path of accumulation, we practice the four mindfulnesses, the first four of the thirty-seven factors of awakening. This is true of the hinayana, mahayana, and vajrayana paths to awakening.

The Tibetan word for mindfulness, *drenpa*, also means "recollection or memory." What is meant by the establishment of recollection, memory, or mindfulness? It means to intentionally use the faculty of recollection, not recollection of the past, but focused attention; hence the use of the English word *mindfulness*. It means to use this faculty intentionally. We use this faculty all the time. We use it to maintain the continuity between picking up food on our forks and putting in our mouths. We couldn't actually do that if we lacked this faculty. We constantly use memory to guide our assessment of the world around us. However, although it is a faculty that we already possess, like many other faculties such as love and compassion and so on, it is one that can still be further developed. The Buddhist approach to the development of mindfulness begins with the focusing of it on four things. The four mindfulnesses are: mindfulness of body, mindfulness of sensations, mindfulness of mind, and mindfulness of dharmas.

Mindfulness of the Body

The practice of mindfulness of the body is a meditation practice in which you sit in meditation posture and with an unaltered and uncontrived awareness observe your body. Now, there are different subtechniques to this, focusing on different parts of the body, focusing on the whole body, and so on. But the idea is a direct and unprejudiced observation of your body.

The purpose is to discover the body's impurity. The discovery of impurity does not mean an obsessive sense of, "oh, my body's filthy; it's unclean; it's gross." You might have such an experience along the way, of course. The idea is the reversal of an illusion. The illusion is the illusion of the body's corporeal purity, an illusion that we strive to maintain. Now, it's never successful; we all know what's inside our bodies. But we go to endless lengths to deny the fact that, other than this thin crust we call skin and flesh, everything in your body is pretty, pretty funky. Before you can start to deal with the body's emptiness, you have to confront the relative truth of the body's impurity. It is a simple thing; you're just trying to be in your body completely. That is enough, because our attempt to convince ourselves that our bodies are pure and eternal and clean and wonderful actually takes us out of our bodies. We actually alienate ourselves from our bodies because we're afraid of the truth. We know deep down; we go to the bathroom every day. We're not fooling anybody. Yet we live in denial of impermanence, and continue to try to convince ourselves that our bodies are other than they are. When we are in romantic relationships we take great pains to maintain that illusion with the other person; we go to enormous lengths to make our bodies seem like sugar and spice within and without, right? Mindfulness of body in the common context consists of letting go of your attachment to the body by being in your body, confronting your body, and experiencing your body. When you do that you gradually start to reverse the illusion of purity or cleanliness.

In the mahayana context, when you do this meditation you analyze the body to determine its emptiness. Rather than looking for the body's impurity you look beyond purity or impurity to see the body's emptiness. You see that "body" is just a label for a certain set or aggregate of things. You analyze your body, break it down into its parts, and break those down into their parts, and so on.

In the vajrayana tradition, the practice of mindfulness of body is the generation stage, in which you visualize your body as the body of the deity. In the case of the common mindfulness of body, you are mindful of your body as it is; in the case of the mahayana mindfulness of body, you analyze the body's components in order to recognize its emptiness; and in the case of the vajrayana mindfulness of body, you meditate on your body as the body of a deity. They all have a common purpose: to realize the body's true nature.

Mindfulness of Sensations

The second type of mindfulness is mindfulness of sensations. In the common form of this technique, it is a simple awareness of physical sensations as they arise. Especially if the emphasis is on tranquility, one particular sensation will be selected for attention, preferably one that is constant or regular; often it is the breathing. Many people have been taught mindfulness of the breath as their first meditation technique.

In the common vehicle, the purpose of mindfulness of sensations is the knowledge of suffering. If practiced persistently, it is said to lead to the discovery that many of your sensations are unpleasant; that the pleasant ones constitute the suffering of change; and that the neutral ones are an aspect of pervasive suffering. The idea here is to discard the illusion that the nature of sensations is inherently pleasant.

In the mahayana form of this, the emphasis is on the recognition of the emptiness of sensations. When a sensation arises, you look directly at it. When you look directly at a sensation, it does not vanish, but it is seen not to have its own separate existence.

The vajrayana technique of mindfulness of sensations is the cultivation of what is called *mahasukha*, or "great bliss," through the completion stage with attributes.

Mindfulness of Mind

It can be practiced in the simplest way as the observation of what arises in the mind. In that case, its purpose is to discover the impermanence of what arises in the mind. Usually, however, the purpose of mindfulness of mind is to discover selflessness.

We very much identify with our minds; whether we regard the mind as a product of the body or the body as merely a temporary dwelling place for the mind, whatever our belief system, we all identify with our minds because we live in our minds. The purpose of this technique is to look at your mind with your mind itself; your mind observes your mind. If you attempt to do this in the sense of one thing looking at another, it is impossible, because a thing cannot look at itself as an object. Your mind has, among its many abilities, one ability that is very important here: self-awareness. Self-awareness, in this context, means that your mind can experience itself. Your eye cannot see itself without a mirror, but your mind can experience itself. We know this to be true in the simplest sense—that we know what we are thinking and what we are feeling. We do not need to ask anyone else. As Khenchen Thrangu Rinpoche often puts it, our own minds are not hidden from us.

In a more subtle way, your mind can actually experience what thinks and what feels by allowing your mind to look at itself. If you do this, your mind's lucidity, its fundamental attribute, will be directed toward itself. We usually direct our mind's lucidity away from itself, as though we believe that our mind's not worth looking at. We ignore the mind itself. This technique is simply to not do that, but to allow the mind's lucidity to settle into itself, to experience itself.

When you allow your mind to look at your mind, you discover what in the common vehicle is called selflessness. You discover that the mind is not a self. Your mind is empty, in that it is empty of any kind of substantial entity. Yet it is a cognitive emptiness; it is a knowing emptiness, a lucid emptiness.

Mindfulness of Dharmas

In this case dharmas are objects of the mental consciousness, both appearances and thoughts. You might ask, "What is the difference between looking at appearances, looking at thoughts, and looking at the mind?" There may not be a difference in the end, but there is certainly a difference in the beginning. Looking at appearances, you simply allow yourself to experience the sense perception of the thing. Usually it's easiest to do this with a visual appearance. You observe the thing long enough that the false distinction between subject and object is worn away. It is worn away only if you do this with sufficient persistence and for a long enough period of time. It is worn away because the border between subject and object is an illusion that requires maintenance. Normally, we only pay attention to a thing for a moment or two. Then we switch to something else. As long as we do that, we can maintain the illusion of our separateness.

I will give you a very simple analogy for this. It is a bit like wearing out our association of the sound of a word with its meaning by repeating the word until its sound seems to be meaningless. It is not exactly the same, because there is a difference between the imputation of the separateness of subject and object and the association of the sound of a word with its meaning. I used to do this as a child as a sort of game; many of you probably did this also. You take a word that is in common use, the meaning of which you know well, and you repeat it until it stops meaning anything. What happens is that your mind becomes tired of supplying the meaning-association with every repetition of the word, and eventually gives up. I can remember doing this until I ended up doubting whether the word I was repeating really existed. This is a little bit similar to what you do when practicing the mindfulness of appearances.

Mindfulness of thoughts can be either just the recognition of thoughts arising and ceasing or looking at the nature of thoughts. The second of these involves looking directly at thoughts as they arise. You observe what the arising of a thought really is, what the presence of a thought really is, and what the disappearance of a thought really is. In other words, you observe whether thoughts actually come from anywhere, whether they really are anywhere while they are present, and whether they go anywhere when they disappear.

These four techniques may be practiced slightly differently in different vehicles. In the common vehicle, their purpose is to reveal impurity, suffering, selflessness, and impermanence; in the mahayana of the sutras, their purpose is to reveal emptiness; and in the vajrayana, they are practiced as the generation stage, the completion stage, and mahamudra.

Questions

STUDENT: Is it necessary to practice all four types of mindfulness?

LAMA YESHE GYAMTSO: I think that any systematic practice of any Buddhist system will include these in one form or another. In our tradition, they are practiced within the four common preliminaries, the four uncommon preliminaries, and the generation and completion stages.

STUDENT: Last night we were discussing faith and devotion. What is the relationship between samaya and devotion?

LAMA YESHE GYAMTSO: According to Karma Chakme Rinpoche, all samaya is included in viewing your guru as inseparable from your yidam, and never giving rise to wrong views toward him or her.

STUDENT: Is most of the suffering that we experience the result of our previous actions?

LAMA YESHE GYAMTSO: Every action is said to have three main results: the fully ripened result, the dominant result, and the concordant result. The concordant result is divided into the result concordant with the cause and the result concordant with the action.

The fully ripened result of any action is the aggregates of a future lifetime. In other words, every significant volitional action in which we engage is the cause of a rebirth in the future. The dominant result is the experience of certain environments in other lifetimes. You can read about the environments caused by various actions in the *Jewel Ornament.* The result concordant with cause is to experience circumstances that concord with that action. For example, if I kill someone, the aggregates caused by that action will probably be birth in a hell realm, but I will also be killed a lot in other lifetimes. The result concordant with the action is the habit of engaging in that action.

THE FOUR VIEWS

We will now look at the four Buddhist philosophical systems. A complete treatment of them would involve looking at every aspect of their views, which we cannot possibly hope to do. What we will try to do this morning is look very briefly at how they view the two truths. The two truths are relative truth and absolute truth. Relative truth is defined by Buddhists as "that which is real for a deluded cognition." A *relative truth* is "whatever is real for the cognition of someone who is not an arya in even placement." An arya or noble is someone who has achieved the path of seeing. Any being who has not achieved the path of seeing is deluded and experiences relative truths as real. This includes all sentient beings who are not on the path as well as those on the lower paths of accumulation and juncture.

Absolute truth is defined as "that which is real for the undeluded cognition of an arya in even placement," so what bodhisattvas in even placement experience as real and what buddhas experience as real at any time—since by definition, buddhas never depart from even placement—is what we would call absolute truth.

The four systems of Buddhist philosophy are: the vaibhashika, the sautantrika, the chittamatra or mind-only, and the madhyamaka or middle way.

Hinayana

The Vaibhashika System

The vaibhashika system is named after the *Mahavaibhasha*, an early commentary on the Abhidharma. It is therefore said to be the system of philosophy based on the Buddha's statements in the Abhidharma of the common vehicle.

The vaibhashika criterion for determining whether something is an absolute or relative truth is this: Anything that can be broken down either physically or analytically is a relative truth. Anything that can be crushed by a hammer or by any actual or hypothetical weight or force is a relative truth. Anything that can be subdivided or broken down by authentic analysis is a relative truth. Therefore the converse is true: anything that cannot be subdivided in any way and that cannot be destroyed or broken down in any way is an absolute truth.

What are the things that withstand this criterion and remain absolute truths? Partless particles and indivisible moments of cognition. According to the vaibhashika system, all matter, if fully analyzed, is composed of indivisible or partless particles. A partless particle is a particle that does not have parts. Because it is not a composite of smaller particles, it cannot be divided or physically destroyed. According to the vaibhashika system, when you break something with a hammer, it breaks because you are separating the particles. You could theoretically keep on doing that, separating the particles into finer and finer bits, until you got down to the partless particles. You could, however, regardless of how much force you exerted, not break or smash these partless particles.

The other principal thing that the vaibhashika system considers to be an absolute truth is indivisible moments of cognition. According to this view, the stream of cognition that we experience as an unbroken continuity of experience, of cognition, is in fact made up of discrete or separate moments. Each of these moments lasts about one sixtieth of the duration of the finger snap of a healthy person, the duration of the sound divided into sixty. According to the vaibhashikas, that is the duration of a cognitive moment or cognitive instant. The vaibhashika contention is that these packets, or discrete moments of cognition, are inherently indivisible. There can be no cognition of briefer duration than that and they assert that you can't meaningfully analyze or subdivide these moments; therefore, they are absolute truths. To put it very roughly, coarse substances that we see are relative truths and the stream of cognition that we experience is a relative truth. The partless particles that are the fundamental building blocks or components of matter and the indivisible moments of cognition that are the building blocks of experience are absolute truths.

The Sautantrika System

The second school, also associated with the common vehicle, is called the sautantrika; this means "sutra followers." They differ from the vaibhashikas in that, rather than favoring the Buddha's statements about reality in the Abhidharma of the common vehicle, they draw their view primarily from the Buddha's statements about reality in the sutras of the common vehicle. They accept the existence of both partless particles and indivisible moments of cognition, but make an important distinction between appearances and hidden objective bases of appearance, which were mentioned yesterday. They assert that the partless particles that make up the hidden objective basis behind an appearance (and also the partless particles that make up my sense organs) are real, but that what I think I see is not real.

These two schools associated with the common vehicle are concerned with breaking down reality to the extent required in order to determine the selflessness of persons. Since their goal is the achievement of the state of an arhat and liberation from samsara, they don't need to go any farther.

Mahayana

The other two systems, the mind-only school and the middle way school, are associated with the mahayana. To attempt to summarize the mind-only school and middle way school presentation of the two truths in a few minutes is ridiculous and disgraceful. However, let us do our best.

The Mind-only School

Generally speaking, the mind-only school asserts that a cognition that is empty of the duality of subject and object is absolute truth and that all other phenomena are relative truths. The appearance of subject and object is dependent on karmic imprints and obscurations; the supposed existence of subject and object is entirely imaginary. The mind-only view is therefore that supposedly indivisible particles and moments of cognition are dependent appearances and their imputed reality imaginary.

The Middle-way school

The middle-way system has many branches, but in general it can be said that middle way adherents accept that only the nature of relative truth is absolute truth. This nature is often described as beyond embellishment, which means that it is not an object of the intellect and cannot be grasped through concepts. However, this does not mean that all middle-way adherents assert that a nature beyond embellishment is absolute truth. In many cases the reasoning employed is strictly reductive and employed solely to demonstrate that any ontological concept whatsoever will ultimately lead to the contradiction of the argument used in advocating it; in such cases no assertions are made.

Some middle way adherents hold buddha nature to be

absolute truth. They say that everything other than buddha nature, the dharmadhatu, is empty of itself; but that the dharmadhatu is empty of everything other than itself, and not empty of its own attributes.

Questions

STUDENT: I have heard Traleg Kyapgon Rinpoche, while teaching mahamudra, advise students to think of things as dependently arisen, and not to worry about whether there is something out there or not. This sounds very similar to sautantrika to me, but I know that the view he is expounding is that of the middle way.

LAMA YESHE GYAMTSO: Most middle way adherents would describe relative truth as dependently arisen. There are also interpretations of the middle way that employ some of the reasoning of the sautantrika. A separate issue is that the Karma Kagyu mahamudra tradition does not emphasize the analysis of external objects. As Khenchen Thrangu Rinpoche has put it, our approach is the direct experience of the nature of all things within our mind. The analysis of external objects is part of taking inferential valid cognition as the path, which is the part of the path of the mahayana of sutra. Because there is a great deal of difference between inference and direct valid cognition, it takes a tremendous amount of accumulation of merit to be able to refine an inference, even a conventionally valid inference, into a direct valid cognition. According to Thrangu Rinpoche, that is why the mahayana path of sutra takes so long.

A key feature, he says, of mahamudra, is that you scrutinize the one thing, among all phenomena, the nature of which can be directly experienced by an ordinary person: one's own mind.

It is often said that one cannot realize the emptiness of anything directly until one achieves the path of seeing. Until that point, one depends on inferential valid cognition alone. According to Thrangu Rinpoche, this is true of all things except one: your own mind. "Anyone who is taught how to do so," he says, and I'm quoting him almost word for word, "can learn to directly experience the emptiness of their own mind." That is why mahamudra is so effective. He also says that once you fully realize the emptiness of any one thing, you have realized the emptiness of everything, because there are no distinctions within emptiness itself.

THE FOUR RELIANCES

We have looked at the four noble truths, the four seals of the view, the four establishments of mindfulness, and the four systems of Buddhist philosophy. We will now discuss the four reliances. The four reliances are one of many ways of explaining how to correctly engage in the path. They are guidelines on how to choose what to study and practice. We cannot study everything about Buddhism; it is limitless. We also cannot engage in every single practice that exists. We must choose what to study and what to practice. The criteria on the basis of which we make these choices are therefore important. You'll remember that in stating the fourth noble truth, the truth of the path, the Buddha said, "Rely on the path; other than the path, there is nothing to be relied upon." You can therefore view the four reliances as a series of choices we face when relying on the path.

Rely on Dharma, not on Persons

This means that you should choose your teachers based on their ability to teach authentic dharma, not based on their appearance, gender, social position, or race. The choice of a teacher cannot be based on the criteria by which you might choose an ordinary friend. It must be based on the effect their teachings have on your mind. If someone's teaching of dharma genuinely helps your mind, beneficially affects your behavior, and weakens your kleshas, you should rely on them.

Rely on the Meaning, not on the Words

We learn the meaning of dharma through the words: the spoken words of the guru and the written words of the Buddha. Just as the guru's persona is simply a container for his or her transmission of dharma, the words of dharma are simply a way to convey the meaning. You are not in it for the words; you are in it for the meaning. The memorization of the words, the acquisition of lists of all kinds that you can spout, is not the proper study of dharma. You must understand the meaning; and to understand the meaning, you have to always emphasize meaning over words.

Rely on the Definitive Meaning, not the Indicative Meaning

The indicative meaning is any statement that, while true, should not be taken literally. The definitive meaning is any statement made by the Buddha that should be taken literally. For example, this is an indicative statement found in one of our liturgies: "Anyone who recites Vajrasattva's mantra even once will purify all obscurations." This statement sounds as though it is saying that immediately upon reciting that mantra once you will be free from all obscurations. What it really means is that by reciting the mantra even once you will form a connection with Vajrasattva that will eventually lead to the purification of all obscurations. The problem that can be caused by failing to understand the true meaning of such a statement is that you might think that a single recitation of Vajrasattva's mantra is enough; that there will be no increased benefit in reciting it more than once. That is not true; if it were, we would not recite such mantras hundreds of thousands of times.

Statements that explain the importance of the realization of the true nature of things, whether it is called emptiness, the clear light, selflessness or whatever, are definitive. Statements about how those are to be realized are usually definitive. Statements that imply that something easy will produce a tremendous traversal of most of the path are usually indicative.

Between the two types of statements it is important, if you have to make a choice, to always choose the definitive meaning over the indicative meaning. However, this does not mean that the indicative meaning is untrue. It is true, but requires interpretation.

Rely on Wisdom, not on Consciousness

This means that we need to transcend the intellect, the conceptual mind. We cannot realize the nature of things solely by using the intellect. It can only be realized by nonconceptual wisdom. This is one reason why compassion and devotion are so important in our path. Compassion is the most effective way to cut through the obsessive selfishness that keeps us so miserable. Devotion is the most effective way to become familiar with buddha nature, our true nature. Attempting to understand our nature conceptually will never work. As Niguma wrote in her *Stages of the Path of Magical Illusion*, "The five paths and ten stages are traversed through devotion."

Questions

STUDENT: How do you know if a rinpoche, a teacher, is for you?

LAMA YESHE GYAMTSO: The traditional criterion is that the teacher who successfully points out the nature of your mind is your root guru. Another way to choose a teacher is to rely upon the guru in whom you have the most faith.

STUDENT: I have a hard time telling the difference between understanding and experience.

LAMA YESHE GYAMTSO: Khenpo Karthar Rinpoche once gave an analogy for the difference between understanding, experience, and realization. He said that if we use the moon as an analogy for buddha nature, the mind's nature, understanding is like seeing a painting of the moon that's accurate enough so that if you thereafter ever actually see the moon, you will know it's the moon. Experience is like seeing a photograph of the moon. Initial realization is like seeing a sliver of the actual moon. Full realization, buddhahood, is like seeing the full moon.

GLOSSARY

ABHIDHARMA: The Buddha's teachings on the nature and attributes of both the external world and the mind.

ABSOLUTE TRUTH: Reality as experienced by the undeluded mind of a Buddha or of a bodhisattva in meditation.

ATIYOGAYANA: The ninth and highest vehicle of Buddhism. It is distinguished by its' transcendence of the intellect.

BODHICHITTA: The mind of awakening, both the intention to achieve awakening and the states of mind cultivated in the process of achieving it.

BRAHMA: A god of the form realm who, along with the god Indra, first requested that the Buddha teach.

BUDDHIST VEHICLES: Spiritual approaches within Buddhism.

CHITTAMATRA OR MIND-ONLY: One of the two principal schools of mahayana philosophy.

EMBODIMENT OF THE THREE JEWELS: A meditation system

focused on Guru Padmasambhava, discovered as treasure in 1620 CE by the vidyadhara Jatsön Nyingpo.

EMPTINESS: The way things really are, not to be confused with nothingness.

EVEN PLACEMENT: Fully stabilized meditation.

GAMPOPA: Milarepa's foremost disciple and the founder of the Kagyu tradition.

HINAYANA: The lesser vehicle, an approach to spiritual practice focused solely on one's own liberation.

INDRA: A god of the desire realm who, along with Brahma, first requested that the Buddha teach.

INSIGHT: Recognition of selflessness or emptiness.

JEWEL ORNAMENT OF LIBERATION: The best-known of Gampopa's writings, an exposition of the mahayana path.

KALACHAKRA: "Wheel of Time," a tantric Buddhist deity.

KARMA AND KLESHAS: Actions and unhealthy emotions, the two proximate causes of suffering.

LUCIDITY OR COGNITION: The mind's ability to know and experience.

MADHYAMAKA OR MIDDLE WAY: One of the two principal schools of mahayana philosophy.

MAHASUKHA: Great bliss.

MAHAVAIBHASHA: An early Indian commentary on the *Abhidharma*.

MAHAYANA: The greater vehicle, an approach to spiritual practice focused on the liberation of others.

NIGUMA'S *STAGES OF THE PATH OF MAGICAL ILLUSION:* An exposition of the tantric spiritual path written by the 11th century female Indian guru Niguma.

NIRVANA: The transcendence of all misery.

PATH OF SEEING: The third part of the Buddhist path. On the path of seeing the nature of all things is seen as it is for the first time.

PATHS OF ACCUMULATION AND JUNCTURE: The first and second parts of the Buddhist path. On the path of accumulation one accumulates merit; on the path of juncture one gradually approaches the wisdom of the path of seeing.

RELATIVE TRUTH: Reality as experienced by the deluded mind of a sentient being or by a bodhisattva not in meditation.

SAMSARA: Spinning, the perennial cycle of suffering and its causes.

SAUTANTRIKA SYSTEM: "Sutra followers," one of the two principal schools of hinayana philosophy.

SEVEN BRANCHES: Seven means of accumulating merit. The seven branches are prostration, offering, confession, rejoicing in virtue, requesting that Buddhadharma be taught, encouraging awakened beings to remain alive, and the dedication of virtue to the awakening of all beings.

SHRAVAKAYANA: TThe vehicle of "the hearers," the first of two lesser vehicles.

TATHAGATHA: "Thus-Gone," a synonym for Buddha.

TRANQUILITY: The ability to rest the mind on a chosen object and the mediation practice that leads to that ability.

TWELVE LINKS OF INTERDEPENDENCE: The twelve progressive stages of samsaric delusion and suffering. They are ignorance; formation; consciousness; name and form; the senses; contact; sensation; craving; attachment; becoming; birth; and aging, sickness, and death.

VAIBHASHIKA SYSTEM: One of the two principal schools of hinayana philosophy.

VAJRAYANA: "Vajra vehicle," tantric Buddhism.

VINAYA: The Buddha's teachings on moral discipline.

VOW OF REFUGE: The vow to always take refuge in the Buddha as a teacher, the Buddhadharma as a path, and the Buddhist sangha as guides on that path.

KTD Publications, a part of Karma Triyana Dharmachakra, is a not-for-profit publisher established with the purpose of facilitating the projects and activities manifesting from His Holiness Karmapa's inspiration and blessings. We are dedicated to "gathering the garlands of the gurus' precious teachings" and producing fine-quality books.

KTD Publications
Woodstock, New York
www.KTDPublications.org

May All Beings Be Happy!